Sarajevo '84

Sarajevo ´84

Imprimé en Suisse, Mars 1984
© C.I.O. – Lausanne; STUDIO 6, Lausanne

Sarajevo ´84

Sarajevo ´84

1
Colourful figures near Baščaršija Square.
2
Artists from all over the country travelled to Sarajevo
for the Games.
3
The Holiday Inn, where the International Olympic
Committee lived.
6
Quaint shops in the Old Town.
7
Local handicrafts.

Sarajevo ´84

1
A permanent presence: the Olympic spirit.
3
The Olympics attract all sorts of people including
John, a familiar figure from Moscow.
4
Vučko, the Games' mascot.

4

Sarajevo ´84

1
The warmth and kindness of a genuinely human atmosphere.
4
The Olympic flame arrives in Sarajevo.

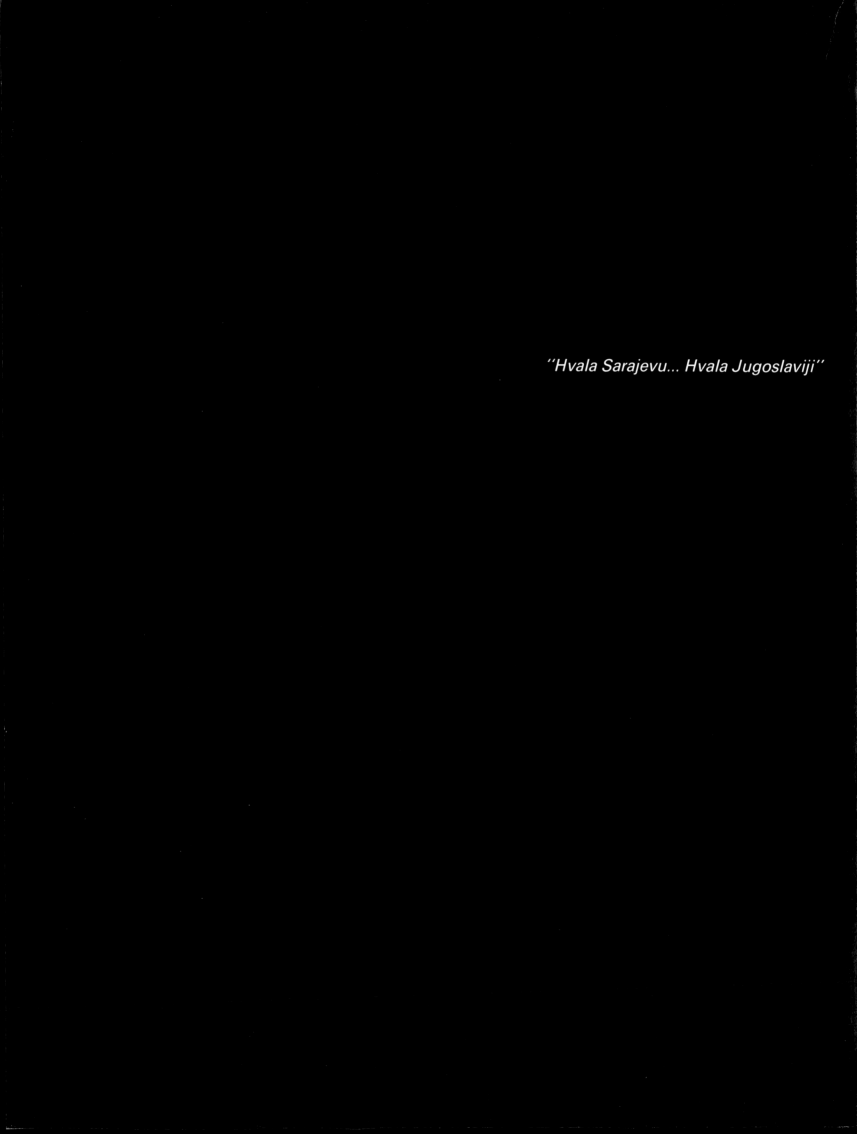

"Hvala Sarajevu... Hvala Jugoslaviji"

Sarajevo ● '84

I am pleased at the opportunity the appearance of this official IOC book on the 1984 Sarajevo Olympics gives me to thank all those who, near and far, contributed to the success of the games.

First, the athletes who gave the best image of themselves and of sport in general, and who, by gathering here at Sarajevo showed that sport and Olympism permit young people from different countries and different political systems to meet and to participate in friendship and fraternity.

I see in that a sign that peace in the world is not impossible. Thanks to the gracious people of Yugoslavia who helped the capital of Bosnia Herzegovina make a success of what must be labelled the biggest and most vibrant exhibition of sport in the world.

Thanks go to the public, either on the spot or thousands of kilometers away, who thrilled to the exploits of its champions thanks to the communications systems that were set up and which sent a wave of enthusiasm around the world shared by all regardless of frontiers. And finally, to the organizers who through their tireless efforts made this occasion a real celebration of sport.

These images of human warmth, of loyal competitions, and of the graciousness of a whole people I will always remember.

This book, the first of a series, retraces these Olympic moments and will give everyone a chance, wherever he may be, to prolong the memory through its illustrations which in themselves are valuable reference documents.

J.A. Samaranch

President
of the International Olympic Committee

Sarajevo '84

This book is a testimony to the great confidence that the IOC placed in Sarajevo and in Yugoslavia as a whole. It demonstrates that we were worthy of this confidence. The organizing committee of the XIVth winter Olympic Games, the city of Sarajevo and Yugoslavia did everything that was necessary to ensure a good organization and that the sites and competition areas were ready for the big day.

We hope that all those who participated in the Games, the tourists and the visitors, all those who came to Sarajevo, were able to enjoy the pleasantness and the sense of hospitality of the people of this region.

The spirit of camaraderie sealed new friendships. Sarajevo and Yugoslavia will do everything to make sure that these friendships and the contacts made are reinforced and enriched.

Our wish is to see our friends again from all over the world an the magnificent slopes of Bjelasnica, Jahorina, Igman and Trebević and to offer them the chance to learn more about our rich history, our culture and the plans of the people of this country.

This book is a testimony to what has happened during the XIVth Olympic winter Games at Sarajevo and we would like it to be a message of warmth and friendship between sportsmen and between the people of the whole world.

Branko Mikulić

Wednesday, February 8, 1984: in the magnificent Kosevo winter stadium, the 14th Winter Olympic Games open before a crowd of spectators estimated at more than 50,000.

8·2·84

" I promise that we shall take part in these Olympic Games respecting and abiding by the rules which govern them, in the true spirit of sportsmanship, for the glory of sport and the honour of our teams. "

Sarajevo ´84

1
Overcome by emotion, Bojan Križaj lost his words
during the Olympic Oath but he soon had his smile
back.
2-3
A colourful world of lights....

Sarajevo ´84

1-12
An extraordinary feeling of warmth and friendliness united the crowd at hand for the opening ceremonies. One nation was host to the world, happy and proud to have risen to the challenge: the Games are declared open and promise to be a memorable homage to sports and international amity.

12

Sarajevo '84

The origins of winter sports are as old as those of other sports. Fragments of skis in Scandinavia and murals dating from the third millennium before Christ are evidence of this ancient heritage.

However the first Winter Olympic Games only date from 1924, thirty years after the decision in Paris in 1894 to create the modern Olympic Games.

It might be assumed that this lag arose from a lack of organization in the practice of winter sport at the turn of the century. But it was nothing of the kind. The International Skating Union, founded in 1892, was part of a group of top international federations such as that representing ice hockey whose foundation dates from 1908. Moreover, during the conference which established the Olympic Games, it was decided to include skating in the programme.

This decision couldn't be applied before 1908 and London at the time of the fourth Olympiad. It was just in time though for the celebrated Ulrich Salchow, the holder of ten world titles, to win the gold medal in figure skating. This discipline was included again for the 1920 Olympics at Antwerp and ice hockey was on the agenda as a demonstration. But let's not get ahead of ourselves.

In 1912 at Stockholm, the Swedes decided not to include skating in the programme of the Games. The Scandinavians weren't keen on having winter sports included because they thought such activities were their special reserve. Since 1901, they had organized, on a four-year basis, the Nordic Games which brought together all the skills on snow and ice existing at the time, including skijoering. These Games were supported by Colonel Victor Balck, the Swedish member of the IOC and a friend of Coubertin.

In 1911 during the IOC session in Budapest, it was proposed to bring the Nordic Games into the Olympic cycle. The motion was widely rejected. Ten years later in Lausanne, the matter was brought up again and in spite of the lack of enthusiasm of Coubertin, it was decided that in January of the year of the 8th Olympic Games in Paris in 1924, an international winter sports week would be organized at Chamonix.

It was a question only of a compromise between Europeans from the North and from the South, but the principle was clearly accepted. The brochures at the time already spoke of the "Winter Games" and in 1925 in Prague, the matter was formalized: The "Chamionarde" Week took on the title "The First Winter Games." In the aftermath, the second went to St. Moritz. The last Nordic Games were held in 1926 and the Scandinavians weren't sorry to see them go because they took the lion's share of honors in the Winter Olympics.

1924-1984: Sixty years have passed and 14 winter games have been held on three continents. Let's briefly trace the stages of this epic which frequently blend with the tales of the various champions and heroes who participated.

Chamonix saw the Norwegian Thorlief Haug, the Nurmi of skis, establish his reputation in two skills: Nordic skiing and the combined. The International Ski Federation was founded on the occasion of the first Games. Its president today is Marc Hodler of Switzerland.

In St. Moritz in 1928, Sonja Henie won the first of three consecutive gold medals in figure skating. The Games attracted 25 countries and more than 500 athletes.

In 1932, the Games crossed the Atlantic for the popular resort at Lake Placid in northern New York State – a gathering spot for screen stars and political celebrities. The Norwegian Birger Ruud became a celebrity himself winning the gold medal in the ski jump. He did it again in 1936 and after the war in 1948 he won the silver medal.

By the time of the fourth Games at Garmisch Partenkirchen, they had reached their maturity. That was due of course to the perfect organization of the Germans, but also to the inclusion of downhill skiing for the men as well as for the women who were equally admired in the Nordic skiing events.

A Norwegian, Ivar Ballangrud won three of the four medals in speed skating.

The Second World War broke the cycle of summer and winter games and the one scheduled for Sapporo in 1940 couldn't take place.

From 1948, the organization of the winter and summer games in the same country ended. St. Moritz was given the Winter Games for the last time.

The ice hockey tournament which was won by the Canadians, was the occasion of a controversy between two national teams from the United States each of whom wanted to be considered the official team. It was only in 1950 that ice hockey was confirmed in the Olympic programme following a reform of the regulations of the International Federation.

In 1952 in Oslo, the Games returned to the cradle of the sport of skiing. The Olympic flame was lit in the home where the first champion of the country Sondre Nordheim was born. Ski jumping took place on the slope in Holmenkollen. In figure skating, Dick Button of England confirmed his victory at St. Moritz.

After the war, downhill skiing grew in importance passing from one combined event to three separate skills. In 1956 at Cortina d'Ampezzo, Toni Sailer reigned supreme with three gold medals. The Russians broke the Scandinavian domination in Nordic skiing winning the relay and taking three of the four races in speed skating.

Television was on the scene too carrying the action and turning winter sports into a truly popular pastime.

In 1960, the resort of Squaw Valley on the state border between Nevada and California was built. Everything happened in the best mountain tradition. The bobsleigh event couldn't be organized. On the other hand, the biathlon for men and speed skating for women were introduced. The Nordic ski events were held at 2,000 metres altitude, a record which didn't prevent the Norwegians, the Swedes and the Finns from equally sharing the medals. The Frenchman Jean Vuarnet was the star of the downhill ski event.

In Innsbruck in 1964, the luge event was introduced as a sixth sport completing the winter programme and giving the Games its present form. The snow was missing but the

VI OLYMPIC WINTER GAMES

14 - 25 FEBRUARY OSLO — NORWAY 1952

HISTORY OF THE WINTER OLYMPIC GAMES

Austrian army transported all that was necessary to the slopes in time. In bobsleigh, the Italian Eugenio Monti won two bronze medals at the age of 36. In 1968, he went off with golds and became a living sports legend. In figure skating, the Calmat-Schnelldorfer duel reached a rare intensity. It ended in favor of the Austrian. The Goitschel sisters exchanged their first and second places on the podium in the slalom and giant slalom while Austrian Toni Sailer was proclaimed the god of skiing.

In Grenoble in 1968, the Winter Games returned to France where they were born. Thirty-seven countries participated a record equalled but never beaten until Sarajevo. Jean-Claude Killy repeated the exploit of Toni Sailer winning three medals in skiing. He became legendary, as did American skater Peggy Fleming whose performances enchanted everyone. The Games were broadcast in colour for the first time.

Asia welcomed the games in 1972 for the first time at Sapporo on the island of Hokkaido in the north of Japan. Before the eyes of a whole country, Yukio Kasaya won the 70-metre ski jump. It was the first gold medal won by a Japanese in the Winter Games. Francisco Fernandez Ochoa did the same for Spain in the special slalom.

Avery Brundage retired at the end of the Munich Games and left his successor Lord Killanin with the prickly problem caused by the withdrawal of Denver which was the designated site for 1976. Innsbruck finally stepped into the breach. The Games were perfectly organized. Rosi Mittermaier just barely missed repeating the exploits of Killy and Sailer. She won two golds and a silver. The Russian team won its sixth consecutive gold medal in ice hockey, a streak which was broken at Lake Placid in 1980.

The 13th Games in that town of 3,500 inhabitants went off magnificently. The People's Republic of China was represented. The American Eric Heiden took five gold medals in speed skating. Ingemar Stenmark and Anne-Marie Moser-Proell had their long careers finally crowned by Olympic gold in the slalom and giant slalom for one and the downhill for the other. In the luge event, Rinn and Hahn of East Germany repeated their gold medal performances of 1976 and following the incredible American victory over the Russians in ice hockey, the Olympic flame was extinguished for another four years until Sarajevo.

2ND OLYMPIC WINTER GAMES

St. Moritz 11-19 th Feb 1928

With the designation in 1978 of Sarajevo for the 14th winter games, a whole region of Europe opened itself to the winter disciplines. At the time of the magnificent opening ceremony, the Olympic flame was carried into the stadium by a Nordic skier heralding the imminent beginning of the competitions. There was a record participation with 49 national committees from five continents. The following pages recall the highlights of the 14th Winter Games.

INTERNATIONAL OLYMPIC COMMITTEE

Sarajevo '84

GOLD MEDAL

Men's downhill
Johnson, William D. - USA
Men's giant slalom
Julen, Max - SUI
Men's slalom
Mahre, Phillip - USA

Women's downhill
Figini, Michela - SUI
Women's giant slalom
Armstrong, Debbie - USA
Women's slalom
Magoni, Paoletta - ITA

DOWNHILL SKIING

SILVER MEDAL	BRONZE MEDAL
Men's downhill Müller, Peter - SUI	**Men's downhill** Steiner, Anton - AUT
Men's giant slalom Franko, Jure - YUG	**Men's giant slalom** Wenzel, Andreas - LIE
Men's slalom Mahre, Steven - USA	**Men's slalom** Bouvet, Didier - FRA
Women's downhill Walliser, Maria - SUI	**Women's downhill** Charvatova, Olga - TCH
Women's giant slalom Cooper, Christin - USA	**Women's giant slalom** Pelen, Perrine - FRA
Women's slalom Pelen, Perrine - FRA	**Women's slalom** Konzett, Ursula - LIE

1
The American William D. Johnson,
gold medal in the downhill.
2
Johnson at the finish.
3
The Austrian Franz Klammer finishes tenth.

Sarajevo '84

Improvising is the main virtue of the people of Sarajevo. The weather disturbances, the forced absences of Hanny Wenzel, Ingemar Stenmark and Marc Girardelli, and the arrival of an unconventional snowfall leads one to suppose that this was a date with chance. And on the surface this appears to be true. But in reality, the six gold medallists represent a sampling which gives credibility to these games at Sarajevo. The availability of the local inhabitants and the liveliness of the sportsmen who were called to the podium complement each other. The gold medals symbolize the Olympic spirit. The diversity sweeps away all doubts.

A complex denied: Paoletta Magoni. She wasn't given much of a chance to win in the special slalom, but she showed considerable determination from the start. Her manner of leaning frantically on the poles going through the first gates showed that she hadn't gotten over the nervous tension inherent in this kind of meeting.

An adaptation to a strange phenomenon: Michela Figini. Nineteen days difference between her and Marie-Therese Nadig in 1972 at Sapporo made her the youngest champion in history, quite simply because her calm character allows her to remove herself from the pressures on her.

A camouflaged philosophy: Debbie Armstrong knows how to be inconspicuous. Even if the giant slalom seemed meant for Erika Hess, she brought a certain easy-going spirit which gave a new value to the Games. Giant killing is part of the Olympic operation.

Steel nerves: Phil Mahre. He had announced long before that the World Cup was an added objective. His objections to the Super-G, his unmistaken attitude towards the high number of competitions in the season cornered him . This quiet American said: "This will by my last season, but I'll finish it with a gold medal."

Psychological intoxication: Bill Johnson won the shortened downhill at Wengen. The weather considerably reduced the value of his success. But he knew that his victory wasn't a one-shot affair. "I feel good in Sarajevo and I'll win." He made his announcement before the downhill with an assurance that irritated a lot of people.

Technical perfection: Max Julen. He was the incarnation of determination. Regularly well placed, he could legitimately claim his title. His honesty compelled him to think of his friend Zurbriggen, the only other one besides Steiner among the top candidates to have participated in all three competitions. The enthusiasm issuing from his gold medal, the first in the history of the Valais, was tarnished by the misadventures of his friend. "You have to try everything in the Games. I failed and that's it." Pirmin Zurbriggen's comment was bitter.

An analysis of these Games at Sarajevo shows that there was something for the pleasure of everyone: the favorites brought into question, the regal competitions, the downhill, all held in one day—a first—and a widespread popular following.

There was another outstanding aspect to the Games and that was the medal won by Jure Franko. It was the first medal won by Yugoslavia in the history of the Winter Games.

As for the six gold medallists, none of them had ever had the honor of taking a place on the highest step of the podium.

Sarajevo ´84

1
Peter Müller of Switzerland,
silver medal in the downhill.
3
The three top finishers in the downhill.
4
Peter Müller.
5
The Australian Steven J. Lee finishes 19th.

5

1
Tomaž Jemc of Yugoslavia finishes 30th in the downhill.
2
The course at Bijelasnica.
4
The Russian Vladimir Makeev, 16th in the downhill.

Sarajevo ´84

1
The Austrian Anton Steiner, bronze medal in the downhill.
2
The Swiss Urs Räber, fifth.
3
Anton Steiner of Austria.
4
The Austrian Helmut Höflehner finishes fifth with the Swiss Urs Räber.

4

Sarajevo ´84

1
Gold medal in the slalom, the American Phillip
Mahre.
2
His twin brother, Steve Mahre, silver medal.
4
Jurij Franko of Yugoslavia.

Sarajevo ´84

1
Steve Mahre.
4
Bojan Križaj of Yugoslavia on his way to a 7th-place
finish.
5
Didier Bouvet, France, bronze medal.

5

Sarajevo ´84

1
Yugoslav supporters heading for the start.
3
Toshihiro Kaiwa of Japan at the start.

Sarajevo ´84

The Swiss Max Julen, gold medal in the giant slalom.

1
Jurij Franko of Yugoslavia, silver medal.
3
Borjan Križaj of Yugoslavia is only a spectator.
4
The Swiss Zurbriggen, a hope which faded.

2

3

4

Sarajevo '84

2
The Egyptian Jamil El Reedy. The true olympic spirit
is in the participation.
3
The American Phil Mahre
finishes eighth in the giant slalom.
4
Andreas Wenzel of Liechtenstein, bronze medal in
the giant slalom.

4

The Swede Niklas Henning finishes 18th in the giant
slalom.

3

Sarajevo ´84

2
The installations for the radio and television commentators.
3
Irene Epple, West Germany.
4
Michela Figini of Switzerland on her way to victory in the downhill.

Sarajevo '84

1
The American Debbie Armstrong,
No. 21,
finishes 21st.
2
The Swiss Maria Walliser,
silver medallist, going all out.

Sarajevo ´84

1
Olga Charvatova of Czechoslovakia, bronze medal.
2
The Australian Marilla Guss is not too unhappy with
her 28th place finish in the downhill.
4
The American Holly B. Flanders.

Sarajevo ´84

2
The Austrian Veronika Wallinger hurtles towards
tenth place.

1
The women's special slalom in the fog.
2
The Swiss Erika Hess finishes fifth.
4
The Italian Paoletta Magoni,
gold medal in the special slalom.

4

1
The Austrian Roswitha Steiner takes fourth place.
2
Ursula Konzett.
3
Ursula Konzett of Liechtenstein, bronze medal.

Sarajevo ´84

1
Perrine Pelen.
3
The emotion of Paoletta Magoni.
4
Perrine Pelen of France, silver medal winner
in the special slalom.

4

4

1
A wonderful surprise: the gold medal in the giant saloim goes to the American Debbie Armstrong.
2
Christin Cooper of the United States, silver medal.
3
Perrine Pelen of France, bronze medal.
4
Following the race, a cameraman with the ABC television network.
5
Serge Lang, one of the great alpine ski specialists.

Sarajevo '84

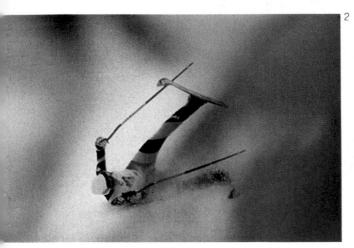

2
Maria Walliser of Switzerland, eliminated in the first
leg of the giant slalom.
3
Perrine Pelen of France.
4
Ursula Konzett of Liechtenstein.
5
Debbie Armstrong.

Sarajevo ´84

1
The American Debbie Armstrong flying towards
victory.
2
A bow.
4
The joy of Debbie Armstrong as she receives the
gold medal.

Sarajevo ´84

1
A Russian competitor going all out in the giant
slalom.

Sarajevo ´84

GOLD MEDAL

Men's
15 km cross-country skiing
Swan, Gunde Anders - SWE
30 km cross-country skiing
Zimiatov, Nikolay - URS
50 km cross-country skiing
Wassberg, Thomas Lars - SWE
4 × 10 km cross-country relay
SWE   Wassberg, Thomas Lars
          Kohlberg, Benny Tord
          Ottosson, Jan Bo Otto
          Swan, Gunde Anders

Women's
5 km cross-country skiing
Hämäläinen, Marja-Liisa - FIN
10 km cross-country skiing
Hämäläinen, Marja-Liisa - FIN
20 km cross-country skiing
Hämäläinen, Marja-Liisa - FIN
4 × 5 km cross-country relay
NOR   Nybraaten, Inger Helene
          Jahren, Anne
          Pettersen, Brit
          Aunli, Berit

70-metre ski jump
Weissflog, Jens - GDR
90-metre ski jump
Nykänen, Matti - FIN

Combined Nordic
Sandberg, Tom - NOR

Biathlon 10 km
Kvalfoss, Erik - NOR
Biathlon 20 km
Angerer, Peter - FRG
Biathlon relay 4 × 7.5 km
URS   Vassiliev, Dimitry
          Kachkarov, Youry
          Shalna, Alguimantas
          Bouliguin, Serguey

NORDIC SKIING

SILVER MEDAL	BRONZE MEDAL

Men's

15 km cross-country skiing
Karvonen, Aki - FIN

30 km cross-country skiing
Zavialov, Alexandre - URS

50 km cross-country skiing
Swan, Gunde Anders - SWE

4 × 10 km cross-country relay
URS   Batuk, Alexandre
       Zavialov, Alexandre
       Nikitin, Vladimir
       Zimiatov, Nikolay

Men's

15 km cross-country skiing
Kirvesniemi, Harri - FIN

30 km cross-country skiing
Swan, Gunde Anders - SWE

50 km cross-country skiing
Karvonen, Aki - FIN

4 × 10 km cross-country relay
FIN   Ristanen, Kari
      Mieto, Juha
      Kirvesniemi, Harri
      Karvonen, Aki

Women's

5 km cross country skiing
Aunli, Berit - NOR

10 km cross-country skiing
Smetanina, Raissa - URS

20 km cross-country skiing
Smetanina, Raissa - URS

4 × 5 km cross-country relay
TCH   Schvubova, Dagmar
      Paulu, Blanka
      Svobodova, Gabriela
      Jeriova, Kvetoslava

Women's

5 km cross-country skiing
Jeriova, Kvetoslava - TCH

10 km cross-country skiing
Pettersen, Brit - NOR

20 km cross-country skiing
Jahren, Anne - NOR

4 × 5 km cross-country relay
FIN   Maatta, Pirkko
      Hyytiainen, Eija
      Matikainen, Marjo
      Hämäläinen, Marja-Liisa

70-metre ski jump
Nykänen, Matti - FIN

90-metre ski jump
Weissflog, Jens - GDR

70-metre ski jump
Puikkonen, Jari - FIN

90-metre ski jump
Ploc, Pavel - TCH

Combined Nordic
Karjalainen, Jouko - FIN

Combined Nordic
Ylipulli, Jukka - FIN

Biathlon 10 km
Angerer, Peter - FRG

Biathlon 10 km
Jacob, Matthias - GDR

Sarajevo '84

Gunde Swan, a native of Dala-Jarna in southern Sweden, participated in his first skiing competition at the age of three.

In 1984, when he wrote a chapter in the history of skiing, Gunde Swan was 22 years old. At Sarajevo, he equalled the Olympic record of his compatriot Sixten Jernberg, one of the idols of Nordic skiing, who won four medals at the Winter Games at Cortina, in 1956. Jernberg took home one gold medal, two silvers and a bronze. Gunde Swan's tally was two golds, a silver and a bronze.

At Sarajevo, during the last overland event, the 50 kilometres, in which Swan was participating for the third time, he was five seconds short of a third gold medal. In the 4 × 10 kilometres relay, Swan easily beat the Soviet champion Nicolai Zimiatov, the golden boy at the Lake Placid Games in 1980.

During the pre-Olympic trials at Sarajevo in 1983, conditions were entirely different from those which prevailed a year later at the time of the Games themselves. At best, conditions could be described as perfect for the Olympics while, in 1983, it was snowing along certain parts of the course, sunny on other parts and raining on others. At that time, Swan finished 25th and was heard to comment: "I went through all four seasons in 15 minutes."

But in 1984, the conditions were the same for everyone.

At the pre-Olympic trials, the Nordic competitors didn't win any of the pure ski events. In 1984, on the other hand, they were vic-torious in seven of the eight competitions; they won two of the three jump competitions and one of three in the biathlon.

Marja-Liisa Hämäläinen added to the Olympic skiing legend by winning the three individual women's events and finishing second in the relay. The 20-kilometre race for women was on the Olympic programme for the first time and in that event, the performance of the Finnish skier was far superior to that of the former queen of overland skiing, Galina Kulakova of the Soviet Union. Aged 28, Marja-Liisa Jämäläinen is a nurse in Jyväskylä in north-eastern Finland.

Whatever, there's no doubt that Harri Kirveseniemi helped bring his fiancée out of anonymity.

The women's team from Norway stood out in the relay. It led from the start. Berit Aunli was the work horse of the team. She is three times world champion and a mother (her husband is another well-known skier Ove Aunli), and her performance at Sarajevo showed that she had successfully made a comeback.

In the combined Nordic event, her compatriot Tom Sandberg defended his world title. It was the first time in a long time that Nordic skiers took all three medals in *their* combination.

Among the other Nordic disciplines, the jump and the biathlon should not be overlooked. Matti Nykänen of Finland and Jens Weissflog of German Democratic Republic dominated the jumping at Malo Polje. The public turned out in record numbers, but unfortunately they didn't see exceptional performances even though they weren't disappointed by the jumps of 20-year-old Nykänen and 19-year-old Weissflog. It won't be forgotten that Nykänen soared for a distance of 116 metres on his first try to break the record on the 90-metre jump. It brought him a total of 231.2 points, 17.5 points ahead of Weissflog.

In the biathlon, Eirik Kvalfoss of Norway and Peter Angerer of West Germany were among the favorites and were up to expectations. Kvalfoss won the 10 kilometres ahead of Angerer who took the 20 kilometres. The Norwegian took third place. Moreover, it was thanks to the 4 × 7.5 kilometres relay that Norway had a silver medal and Federal Republic of Germany a bronze. They couldn't do anything against the Soviet Union which won this event for the fifth time in a row since its introduction in the Olympic Games at Grenoble in 1968.

1
Peter Angerer (FRG), biathlon gold medal.
2
Presentation of the biathlon medals: Angerer,
Roetsch and Kvalfoss.
3
An incident during the running of the biathlon.

1
The favorite, Ullrich (GDR), at the finish line.
He finished only in fifth place.
2
The Korean Whang on his way to 60th place in the
biathlon.
3
Kinoshita of Japan going full out. His effort takes
him to 39th place.
4
Ullrich taking aim.
5
The Russian Vassiliev. He finished 32nd.

5

1
On the road to the 15 km track.
2
Ricardo Holler of Argentina.
3
Harri Kirvesniemi of Finland striding to a bronze
medal in the 15 km.
4
Gold medal winner in the 15 km,
Gunde Anders Swan of Sweden.
5
Unnamed racer.

1

The intensity of the 10 km biathlon.

Sarajevo ´84

1
In the 4 × 10 kilometres, the Swede Gunde Anders
Swan in pursuit of the Russian competitor.
2
The Finn Juha Mieto whose team won the bronze
medal in the 4 × 10 kilometres.
3
The Swedes celebrating their medal.

5

Sarajevo ´84

1
Marja-Liisa Hämäläinen.
2
Raïssa Smetanina of the Soviet Union,
silver medal in the 10 kilometres.
3
A great champion, M.L. Hämäläinen of Finland.
4
Nikola Lavery of Britain finishes 46th
in the 10 kilometres.
5
Marie Lillemor Risby of Sweden at the finish line of
the 5 kilometres in which she finished 4th.

Sarajevo ´84

2
R. Smetanina of the Soviet Union,
silver medal in the
20 kilometres, after winning the
silver medal in the
10 kilometres.

1

2

1
Guidina Dal Sasso of Italy
at the finish line in the 20 kilometres.
She finished 10th.
3
Norwegian supporters.
4
Brit Pettersen of Norway.

Sarajevo ´84

2
The Finn Puikkonen. The joy of the bronze medal.
3
Nykaenen, Finland, silver medal in the 70-metre ski jump event.
4
A great champion: The East German Jens Weiss-flog, gold medal.

Sarajevo ´84

1
Andreas Bauer of West Germany.
2
Fifth in the 70-metre ski jump event: the Norwegian
Rolf Aage Berg.
3
Unable to control his enthusiasm, a spectator
throws himself in the snow.

3

Sarajevo ´84

2
Matti Nykaenen of Finland, gold medal in
the 90-metre jump with a record jump
of 116 metres.
3
Nykaenen, the triumph.

Sarajevo ´84

1
Jens Weissflog, German Democratic Republic,
silver medal.
3
After the fall, an unexpected meeting between a
judge and a jumper.
4
Klaus Ostwald, German Democratic Republic, 26th.

Sarajevo '84

1
Tom Sandberg, Norway,
gold medal in the Combined Nordic.
2
The Finn Jukka Ylipulli, bronze medal.
3
A brilliant race for Jouko Karjalainen of Finland,
winner of the silver medal.
4
Glimpses of the course.

3

4

5

Sarajevo ´84

GOLD MEDAL

Pairs figure skating
Valova, Elena - URS
Vassiliev, Oleg

Ice Dancing
Torvill, Jayne - GBR
Dean, Christopher

Men's figure skating
Hamilton, Scott - USA

Women's figure skating
Witt, Katarina - GDR

FIGURE SKATING

SILVER MEDAL	BRONZE MEDAL
Pairs figure skating Carruthers, Kitty - USA Carruthers, Peter	**Pairs figure skating** Selezneva, Larissa - URS Makarov, Oleg
Ice Dancing Bestemyanova, Natalya - URS Boukin, Andrey	**Ice Dancing** Klimova, Marina - URS Ponomarenko, Serguey
Men's figure skating Orser, Brian - CAN	**Men's figure skating** Sabovtchik, Jozef - TCH
Women's figure skating Sumners, Rosalyn - USA	**Women's figure skating** Ivanova, Kira - URS

Sarajevo ´84

Sarajevo ´84

Sarajevo '84

Tiffany Chin now 16, got her chance to take part in the Olympics in 1984 finished fourth.

Tiffany started out in twelfth place in the school figures but was second only to the eventual winner, Katarina Witt of East Germany, in the short programme section, and third behind Kati and Tiffany's teammate, Rosalynn Sumners, in the final portion.

The women's event was, as expected, a dual between Kati, the twice European champion, and Roz, the 1983 world champion. The American gained an initial advantage winning the school figures in which competitors slowly trace circles on the ice without music, which is worth thirty percent of the contest. Kati was third in the figures but overtook Roz after the short programme division in which the skaters execute seven set moves in any order to their own choice of music. While Kati skated flawlessly in this portion. Roz was forced to put her second foot on the ice to keep her balance after landing in the double axel jump.

The battle between the 18-year-old from Karl Marx Stadt and the 19-year-old from a suburb in Seattle echoed the 1980 event in which Anett Poetzsch of East Germany triumphed over Linda Fratianne, USA.

The decision was extremely close with five judges voting for the East German and four for the American. Kati said later that she admired Roz's artistry but thought the decision had gone in her favour because she had executed more triple rotation jumps.

Kati had started her four minute routine with a combination of two jumps, double lutz to triple

toe loop, and later brought off a triple salchow and triple toe loop. Roz had accomplished a triple toe loop and salchow but left out her triple combination.

The judges' job was made slightly easier because two had drawn to skate together, the raspberry attired Kati next to last and then Roz, dressed all in white with a V of turquoise sequins around her neck. There were a record number of sixes in the ice dance contest which has only been part of the Olympic schedule since 1976.

The King and Queen of this sport were, without doubt, Jayne Torvill and Christopher Dean, from Nottingham (centre of England).

The 26-year-old Jayne and the 25-year-old Christopher gave notice right from the opening round that they were in a class by themselves. In the third compulsory dance, the Westminster Waltz, they were given three 6.0s.

Their next round, the Original Set Pattern Dance, which, for the 1983-84 season, was to a specified Paso Doble rhythm, gained them yet more sixes.

The free dance took place on Valentine's Day, Tuesday February 14th. Attired in varying shades of purple and using Ravel's "Bolero" for their entire four minutes.

They were greeted by three sixes for their first set of marks and straight sixes for the second. There has only been one other occasion in the history of all four divisions of figure skating in which a complete flush of sixes has been given. That was in the 1983 World championships and was for Jayne and Christopher's circus oriented "Barnum" free dance.

In 1980 Jayne and Chris-

topher were fifth in the Olympics as was Scott Hamilton, USA. Scotty's growth was stunted in childhood and he is only 5'3" and 110 pounds. However he has the charisma of a true star.

Although Scotty, who is 25 and now lives in Denver, was overshadowed in both free skating portions by Brian Orser of Canada, even Brian refers to Scott as a true champion. While Scott won the school figures and came second in the short and long programmes sections, Brian had lost too much ground initially when he was seventh in the figures, to challenge Scott seriously.

Like Scott, Elena Valova and Oleg Vasiliev, from Leningrad, won their event with performances which were not their best. The Olympics entail so much pressure that it is only the rare performer who does not suffer from tremendous nerves. Elena, who is 21, and Oleg, 24, made slight errors and their performance was not as good as when they won the European championship four weeks previously. However it was sufficient for all nine judges to give them their top marks in both parts of the pair championship. Soviet skaters have now won all Olympic pairs titles since 1964.

The US champions, Kitty and Peter Carruthers, benefited by mistakes made by the East German and Canadian champions who had gained second and third in the 1983 World championship. The Americans skated a flawless free programme and although they did not demonstrate their extremely difficult triple toe loop and double axel solo jumps which the Russians did so well, they were able to win the silver medals.

Sarajevo ´84

1
Pairs, Kitty Carruthers and Peter Carruthers,
silver medal.
2
The American Mark Cockerell, 13th.
3
Norbert Schramm,
German Democratic Republic, 9th.
4
Ice dancing: Carol Fox and Richard Dalley of the
United States, 5th

5
Tiffany Chin of the United States, 4th.
6
Kira Ivanova of the Soviet Union, bronze medal.
7
The Canadian Brian Orser, silver medal.

Sarajevo '84

1
Gold medal in ice dancing, Jayne Torvill and
Christopher Dean.
2
Pairs, Elena Valova and Oleg Vassiliev, gold medal.
4
Sabine Baess and Tassilo Thierbach, 4th in the
pairs.

Sarajevo ´84

2
Katarina Witt, German Democratic Republic,
gold medal.
3
Rosalyn Sumners, United States, silver medal.
4
Grzegorz Filipowski, Poland, 12th. A young hope of
seventeen years.

Sarajevo '84

2

3

1
The fantasy of Scott Hamilton, gold medal.
2
In pairs: Bo Luan and Bin Yao, People's Republic of
China, finish 15th.
4
Barbara Underhill and Paul Martini, Canada,
7th in the pairs.

4

1
Larissa Selezneva and Oleg Makarov of the Soviet
Union, bronze medal in the pairs.
2
Claudia Massari and Leonardo Azzola,
German Democratic Republic, 13th in the pairs.
3
Alexander Fadeev of the Soviet Union, 7th.

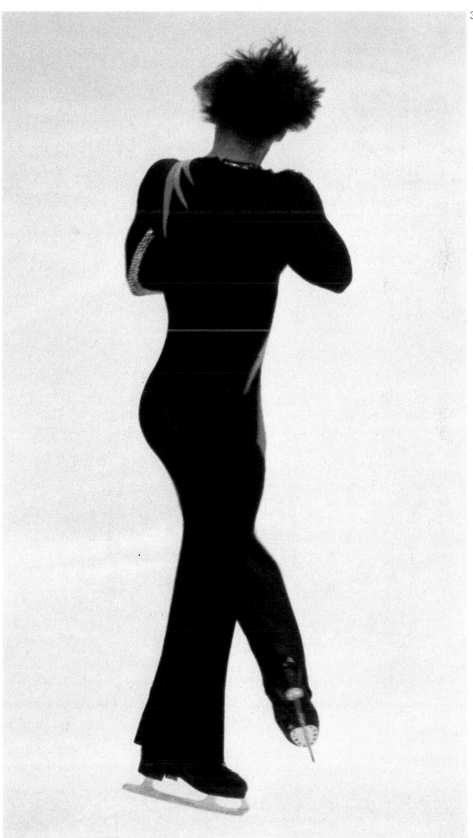

Sarajevo ´84

2
The joy of Katarina Witt, gold medal.
3
Christophe J. Simond of France, 6th.

1
Jayne Torvill and Christopher Dean of Britain,
gold medal winners in ice dancing.
2
The silver medal to Natalya Bestemyanova
and Andrey Bukin of the Soviet Union.

2

Sarajevo ´84

1
Jae-Hyung Cho, 23rd.
3
Susan Jane Garland and Ian Roger Jenkins
of Britain, 14th in the pairs.
4
Elena Vodorezova of the Soviet Union, 8th.
5
The Canadian Jaimee Eggleton, 20th.

Sarajevo ´84

GOLD MEDAL

Speed skating
500 m men
Fokitchev, Serguey - URS
1000 m men
Boucher, Gaëtan - CAN
1500 m men
Boucher, Gaëtan - CAN
5000 m men
Gustafson, Sven Tomas - SWE
10 000 m men
Malkov, Igor - URS

500 m women
Rothenburger, Christa - GDR
1000 m women
Enke, Karin - GDR
1500 m women
Enke, Karin - GDR
3000 m women
Schöne, Andrea - GDR

SPEED SKATING

SILVER MEDAL	BRONZE MEDAL
Speed skating	**Speed skating**
500 m men	**500 m men**
Kitazawa, Yoshihiro - JPN	Boucher, Gaëtan - CAN
1000 m men	**1000 m men**
Khlebnikov, Serguey - URS	Engelstad, Kai Arne - NOR
1500 m men	**1500 m men**
Khlebnikov, Serguey - URS	Bogiev, Oleg - URS
5000 m men	**5000 m men**
Malkov, Igor - URS	Schöfisch, René - GDR
10000 m men	**10000 m men**
Gustafson, Sven Tomas - SWE	Schöfisch, René - GDR
500 m women	**500 m women**
Enke, Karin - GDR	Chive, Natalya - URS
1000 m women	**1000 m women**
Schöne, Andrea - GDR	Petrousseva, Natalya - URS
1500 m women	**1500 m women**
Schöne, Andrea - GDR	Petrousseva, Natalya - URS
3000 m women	**3000 m women**
Enke, Karin - GDR	Schönbrunn, Gabie - GDR

Sarajevo '84

Speed-skating enthusiasts have every reason to remember Sarajevo with pleasure. First of all, there is the oval itself, in the magnificent Zetra ice complex. Superbly laid out and upkept, it led more than one observer to predict, even before the Games opened, that it would generate miracles.

While that did not prove true in the men's events, with Olympic records — all Eric Heiden's 1980 performances at Lake Placid — holding firm, the women's competitions were an altogether different matter. In the 500 metres, four contestants broke Karin Enke's world record including the titleholder herself while five did the same in the 1,000 m race, led, as expected, by Karin Enke.

She didn't stop there, either, going on to beat Natalya Petruseva of the Soviet Union in a memorable race in which no less than 12 racers broke the Olympic mark.

The 3,000 metres was another thrilling event for everyone who saw it. Here again, the current Olympic record was beaten twice. So in 1984 women athletes provided many of the exceptional moments in speed skating. Sports enthusiasts on hand in Sarajevo were perfectly aware of the fact, too, excitedly crowding around the Zetra speed ring.

If Lake Placid will long be remembered for Eric Heiden's exploits, Sarajevo's contented spectators surely cherish durable memories of Karin Enke's remarkable achievements.

Her trainers agree that she was particularly well prepared for Sarajevo. Initially attracted to figure skating (at 16 she was considered the world's finest jumper),

Karin Enke placed ninth at the European championships in 1977. Her build, 1.75 m for 72 kg, does of course constitute a decided advantage for speed skating. A native of Dresden, she turns 23 this year.

Also from Dresden, Christa Rothenburger, 24, won the gold medal in the 500-metre race in 41.02 seconds, not quite up to her own world record of 39.69 seconds, set in 1983. In fact, the entire GDR team made a strong impression, its string of victories demonstrating undeniable collective superiority.

Coming back to the men's events, Montreal marketing student Gaëtan Boucher created quite a stir. Not that he was totally unknown but no one had realised that he could be so effective over short distances. At Sarajevo, along with taking the bronze in the 500-metre event, he collected gold in the 1,000 and the 1,500 races. While the gold won by Sergei Fokitchev of the Soviet Union was not really a surprise, the silver medal which Yoshihiro Katazawa took back to Japan made more than one observer sit up and take notice.

All in all, the suspense, upsets and victories at Sarajevo rekindled spectator interest in what is clearly an important sport at the Winter Olympics, representing no less than 27 medals.

1
N. Petrousseva of the Soviet Union, bronze medal in the 1,500 metres.
2
The three medal winners in the 1,500 metres.
3
A trainer following the efforts of his racers.

1
The speed skating track at Zetra.
3
Competitor going all out.
4
The Yugoslav Behudin Merdović
in the 5,000 metres.
5
The Russian skater Koulechova,
fourth in the 500 metres.
6
Preparing the track.
7
Presentation of the medals: Gold, C. Rothenburger,
East Germany; Silver, K. Enke, East Germany;
Bronze, N. Chive, Soviet Union.

8
The Swede Sven Tomas Gustafson, gold medal in
the 5,000 metres.
9
Gaëtan Boucher of Canada, bronze medal in the
500 metres.

9

1
Gaëtan Boucher of Canada,
gold medal in the 1,000 metres.
2
Olga Plechkova of the Soviet Union,
forth in the 3,000 metres.
3
Gaëtan Boucher, Canada.
4
Hans Sture Magnussen of Sweden
in the 1,000 metres.

4

Sarajevo ´84

1
Silver medal to Serguey Khlebnikov
of the Soviet Union in the 1,000 metres.
2
Karin Enke, winner of no less than four medals
in speed skating.
3
Karin Enke, East Germany, silver medal
in the 3,000 metres.

Sarajevo ´84

1

2

3

2
The 1,500 metres in the magnificent surroundings
of Zetra.
3
Björn Nyland of Norway on his way to a 13th-place
finish in the 10,000 metres.

Sarajevo '84

GOLD MEDAL

Two-man bob
GDR II Hoppe, Wolfgang
         Schauerhammer, Dietmar
Four-man bob
GDR I Hoppe, Wolfgang
         Wetzig, Roland
         Schauerhammer, Dietmar
         Kirchner, Andreas

Presentation of the gold medals in the four-man bob event.

SILVER MEDAL

Two-man bob
GDR I   Lehmann, Bernhard
         Musiol, Bogdan
Four-man bob
GDR II   Lehmann, Bernhard
         Musiol, Bogdan
         Voge, Ingo
         Weise, Eberhard

BRONZE MEDAL

Two-man bob
URS II   Ekmanis, Zintis
         Aleksandrov, Vladimir
Four-man bob
SUI I   Giobellina, Silvio
         Stettler, Heinz
         Salzmann, Urs
         Freiermuth, Rico

Sarajevo '84

This exciting sport speciality is the oldest of the contemporary ice sports and had always been dominated by the Swiss, the Italians, the British and even the Rumanians. But today, the Germans of German Democratic Republic have studied the techniques of bobsleigh building, aerodynamics and the friction of the blades on the ice and have found a new design permitting them to obtain astounding results. These machines were the big surprise at Sarajevo.

What's more, the racers are extremely well trained. They are total athletes who know how to push their bob at the start with the kind of energy that gains them precious hundredths of a second to give them victory. And even when another team gets the jump at the start, the superiority of the East German sled makes up for lost time.

Wolfgang Hoppe was a veritable virtuoso who drove both the two-man and four-man bobs to a victory that no one could contest.

The Germans of German Democratic Republic were Olympic champions at Innsbruck in 1976 and at Lake Placid in 1980, and at Sarajevo they didn't let anyone take the first two places. Now, with Hoppe, the German Democratic Republic has a champion with a long future. It was only two and a half years ago that he started in the discipline and he is already a great. In any case, if he is unseated as the king of bobsledders, one of his compatriots will be.

The Swiss, with Silvio Giobellina, probably the best pilot in the world, felt the difference between the run at Trebevic and the ones at St. Moritz, Villars, Cortina and others where they are used to race. And of course there was also the difference in machines. The bob and the luge events at Sarajevo enjoyed the biggest popular success in their history. Each day, more than twelve thousand spectators crowded round the edges of the run.

1
Gold Medal, the East German bob: Wolfgang
Hoppe and Dietmar Schauerhammer.
2
The need for absolute concentration.
4
The icy environment of the bob at Trebević.

1
England II: loneliness at 110 kilometres an hour.
2
Aerodynamics in the quest for speed.
3
The duel of the giants.
The silver medal to East Germany I.
4
The Soviet bob, bronze medal.

4

Sarajevo ´84

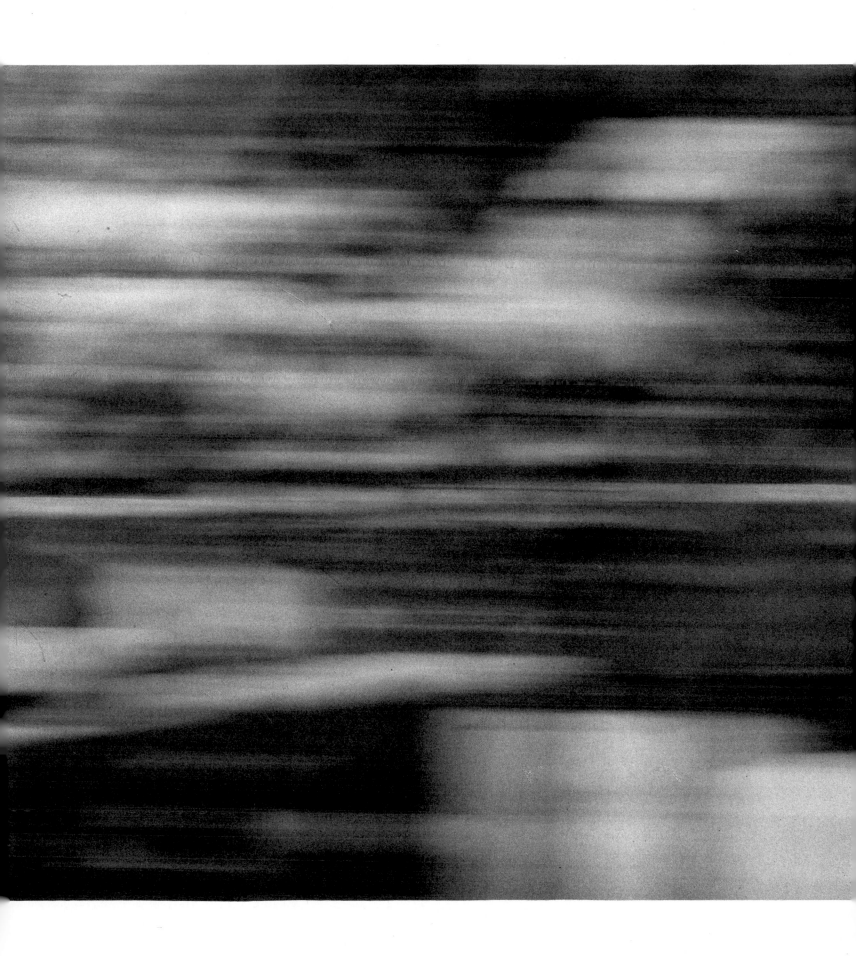

Sarajevo ´84

2
The Swiss bob prepares to leave. It won a bronze medal.
3
The second team of German Democratic Republic, silver medal.

4

Sarajevo ´84

GOLD MEDAL

Women's single luge
Martin, Steffi - GDR

Men's single luge
Hildgartner, Paul - ITA
Men's double luge
FRG   Stangassinger, Hans
        Wembacher, Franz

SILVER MEDAL	BRONZE MEDAL

Women's single luge
Schmidt, Bettina - GDR

Women's single luge
Weiss, Ute - GDR

Men's single luge
Danilin, Serguey - URS
Men's double luge
URS   Beloussov, Evgueny
         Belyakov, Alexandar

Men's single luge
Doudin, Valerij - URS
Men's double luge
GDR   Hoffmann, Joerg
         Pietzsch, Jochen

LUGE

Sarajevo '84

The oldest vehicle known to man continues to bring pleasure to racers in alpine countries. At Sarajevo, an Italian policeman, Paolo Hildgartner, was supreme in the single luge event, skilfully shaving hundredths of a second off each run down the track at Trebevic and undeniably asserting himself. He owed it to himself to regain his Olympic title in the double luge which he had won 12 years before in Sapporo with his compatriot Valter Plail.

Hildgartner is a man devoted to the luge. He doesn't restrict himself to racing and winning. He studies, calculates and designs the best luges so that the children of Ehrenburg, in northern Italy, can participate in their favorite sport.

At the Trebevic run, Hildgartner succeeded in staying ahead of the Russian lugers, who in the first legs always took the lead thanks to the superb physical conditioning of Danilin and Doudin. But Hildgartner knew how to cut a corner and follow the ideal line to win the first Olympic medal on this run. He was nearly half a second faster than the two Russians.

In the double luge event, it was another story. With this sled, other factors such as the coordination of movements, the double push at the start and... the absence of Hildgartner entered into the matter.

The Germans of German Democratic Republic took pitiless revenge winning by a considerable margin. The two German sleds dominated from start to finish. The only opponent who was able to threaten them was the Soviet Union. But the Russians weren't able to manoeuvre suf-

ficiently easily over the short run and, at the finish, the times of Hoppe and Lehman were still the best.

It should be said too that the Germans haven't lost since the Winter Games at Innsbruck in 1976.

In spite of the notable progress of the Russians, they have never won a medal. The Austrians were expected to do well as one of the great countries in the fragile two-man sleds, but they haven't yet regained their former supremacy.

The important name among women lugers is the 22-year-old German Steffi Martin. She raced four legs faultlessly combining daring with remarkable physical conditioning. No one can deny the supremacy of this well proportioned specialist. Her compatriots, Bettine Schmids and Ute Weiss; confirmed that in East Germany, the luge is almost a national sport. They took three first places and even the Olympic champion at Lake Placid in 1980, Vera Zozoulya of the Soviet Union had to yield 12 hundredths of a second.

1
T. Guerlitzer (GDR).
2
Bonny Warner, American women luger,
going full out.

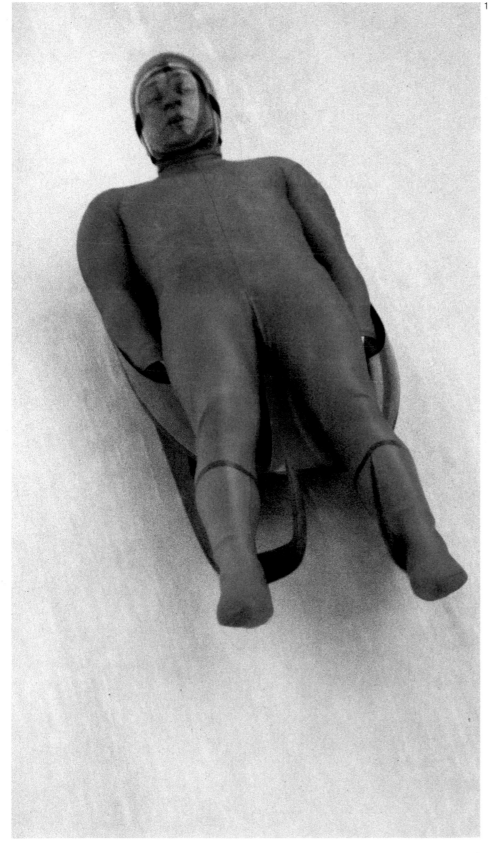

1
Yumiko Kato of Japan, going into a turn.
2
The attraction of the luge for children.
3
The American Frank Masley, finishing his run.

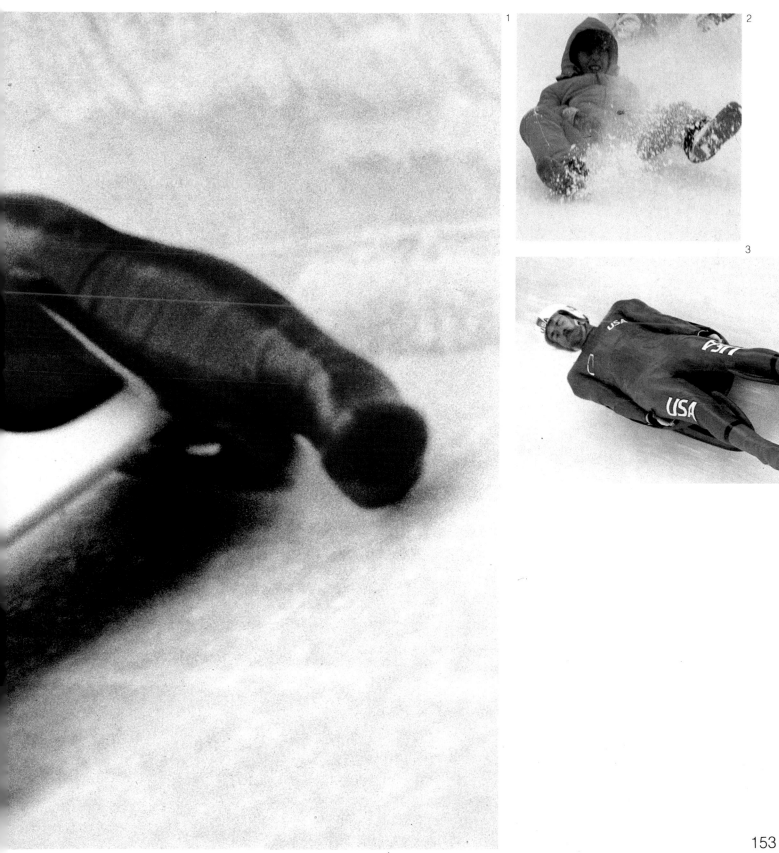

Sarajevo ´84

1
H. Stangassinger and F. Wembacher, of the Federal
Republic of Germany, gold medal winners in the
double luge event.
2
Stangassinger and Wembacher speeding to victory
in the double luge event.

Photos Keystone

2

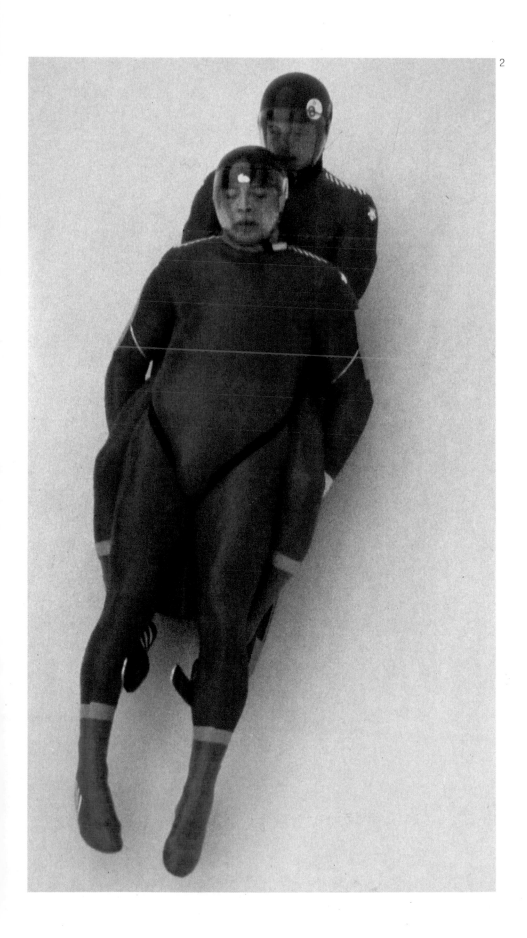

Sarajevo ´84

GOLD MEDAL

Ice Hockey

URS
Bilialetdinov, Zenetoula
Chepelev, Serguey
Drozdetskiy, Nikolay
Fetissov, Viatcheslav
Guerassimov, Alexandre
Kassatonov, Aleksey
Khomoutov, Vladimir
Kovin, Vladimir
Kozhevnikov, Alexandre
Kroutov, Vladimir
Larionov, Igor
Makarov, Serguey
Michkin, Vladimir
Pervoukhin, Vassily
Skvortsov, Alexandre
Starikov, Serguey
Stelnov, Igor
Tretyak, Vladislav
Tumenev, Victor
Vasilev, Mikhail

HOCKEY

SILVER MEDAL

Ice Hockey
TCH   Benak, Jaroslav
Caldr, Vladimir
Chalupa, Milan
Horava, Miloslav
Hrdina, Jiri
Kadlec, Arnold
Korbola, Jaroslav
Kralik, Jiri
Kyhos, Vladimir
Lala, Jiri
Liba, Igor
Lukatch, Vincent
Paschek, Duschan
Richter, Pavel
Rusnak, Darius
Ruzsitchka, Vladimir
Schindel, Jaromir
Svoboda, Radoslav
Tchernik, Frantischek
Uvira, Eduard

BRONZE MEDAL

Ice Hockey
SWE   Ahlen, Thomas Valter
Ekland, Thom Lennart
Eklund, Per-Erik
Ericsson, Bo
Eriksson, Lars Elias
Gradin, Peter Olof
Hessel, Mats Gunnar
Hjalm, Peter Michael
Lindblom, Göran Folke
Motrh, Tommy Jean
Nordin, Leif Hakan
Ohling, Jens Erik
Riddervall, Rolf Lennart
Rundquist, Thomas Valter
Sandström, Tomas
Södergren, Karl Hakan
Thelin, Mats Gunnar
Thelven, Arne Michael
Walitalo, Göte Emil
Waltin, Mats Stefan

Sarajevo '84

If there had ever been a more masterly exhibition of hockey then was displayed by the Soviet team in Sarajevo, no one could remember it. Led by their indomitable goaltender, Vladislav Tretiak, the Russians played as if they were out to prove they were not just the best team in the XIVth Winter Olympics, but the best hockey team in the history of the sport. They may have done so. In seven games, the Soviets outscored their opponents 48-5, breezing through the medal round against the surprising Canadians and powerful Czechoslovakians without allowing a single goal. The tenor of the competition was aptly set by Tretiak two days before the opening ceremonies, when he skated up to a startled journalist who was watching the Soviet practise and said. In English, "We very good. We very *hungry.*"

These were Tretiaks's fourth, and final, Olympics. He was nineteen when he won his first Gold Medal at Sapporo in 1972, and since that time he has become the very symbol of international hockey competition, as beloved in Montreal as he is in Moscow. He has played in, and won, all the great tournaments—the Canada Cup, the World Championships, the Izvestia Cup. But to Tretiak, none of them compared to the Olympic Games in importance. "It is the spirit of competition among the athletes," Tretiak had said last March in his Moscow apartment. "Nowhere else can you live in a village with the other sportsmen, to see what they are like, to share this thing that we all have between us. It is a very special feeling." Then, in a bookcase full of trophies. Tretiak turned to his Olympic Medals first.

"Here are my two Golds, here is my Silver..." Then on and on and on.

Ah, the Silver. It surprised me a little that Tretiak did not have that locked in a trunk in the cellar, for it reminded him of the 1980 Olympics in Lake Placid, when the Soviets were beaten out of the Gold Medal by the young team from the United States. For four years Tretiak and his teammates and coaches had lived with the memory of that shocking upset, and they came to Sarajevo looking forward to a rematch. Alas, it was not to be. Seeded in Group B, the United States team disappointed nearly everyone by losing its first two games to Canada and Czechoslovakia, then tying Norway, eventually finishing in seventh place with a record of 2-2-2. "All year long our heads were filled with hopes and dreams of defending the Gold Medal," said one of the U.S. players. "But when reality settled in, we were lost."

As expected, the strong Czech team finished in first place in Group B with a perfect record of five wins, no losses. Canada, with its tenacious defense, also advanced to the medal round, losing only to the Czechs, a 4-0 shutout. The Canada-Czech game was probably the roughest in the tournament, a contest filled with bruising bodychecks and fine goaltending. Finland clinched third place in the division when they tied the United States, 3-3, with a goal in the final 21 seconds of their match. The Finns' most surprising feat, however, took place, not on the ice, but in the doping control center, where four of their hockey players consumed fifty beers after one game, earning a mild rebuke from Olympic officials.

In Group A, the big news was that the Yugoslav hockey team recorded its first-ever Olympic victory, a 5-1 win over Italy that sent Sarajevans singing in the streets. Sweden and West Germany battled to a 1-1 tie, both finishing 3-1-1- within the division. Sweden, however, advanced to the medal round on the basis of goal differential—this despite a 10-1 loss to the Russians. After that game Swedish Coach Anders Parmstroem shook the hand of Soviet coach Viktor Tikhonov and said, "Thanks for the lesson."

Indeed, it seemed sometimes as if the Russian team was putting on a clinic rather than competing for a medal. Before Canada played the Soviet Union in the medal round, Canadian coach Dave King said: "It's good experience for our kids to face the Russians at this stage in their careers. We're just learning our trade; the Soviet players have mastered theirs. Our guys will learn what a long way they have to go. Mind you, we're not quite raising the white flag yet."

They certainly didn't. Halfway through the Canada-Russia game, the score was tied, 0-0 when Tretiak, who had had little to do, made a sparkling save on a breakaway. The game suddenly turned. A minute and a half later the Soviets scored their first goal, and they coasted in with a 4-0 win.

Sweden, which had been beaten by Czechoslovakia in the other medal round game, went on to win the Bronze Medal on Sunday by shutting out the gritty Canadians, 2-0. It marked the third straight game that Canada had failed to score. But all attention was now focused on the Czech-

The Soviet goalie Vladislav Tretyak:
four Olympic Games, four medals.

The Soviet goalie Vladislav Tretyak:
four Olympic Games, four medals.

Russian final that would determine the Gold Medal, fought between the only two unbeaten teams in the tournament.

Both teams played conservatively, but the Russians took an early lead when a shot by Alexander Kozkevnikov struck the crossbar and then bounded into the net off the arm of Jaromir Schindel, the wonderful Czech goalie. In the second period Vladimir Kroutov made the score 2-0 when he took a sprawling, falling-down pass from Igor Larionov and fired it home. That ended the scoring. The Czechs, showing great heart, continued to press the attack for the rest of the game, but the Russians always seemed to have one extra man around the puck. The few times the Czech forwards could penetrate the great Russian defense of Viatcheslav Fetissov and Aleksey Kassatonov—who may be the finest defense pair in the history of hockey—Tretiak was there to stop them. When the Gold Medal was placed around Tretiak's neck in the awards ceremony that followed, it marked the first time in the history of the Winter Olympics than an athlete had won a medal in four separate Games.

Asked afterwards if the Soviets' showing at Sarajevo atoned for its loss at the Lake Placid Games, Soviet coach Tikhonov said, "In sport one must always look forward. This concerns not only losses, but wins as well. Lake Placid is history. Now Sarajevo, too, is history, and we must look forward to new games and new stars."

It is for coaches to say such things. For the rest of us, there will never be a new star with quite the radiance of Vladislav Tretiak.

Sarajevo ´84

1
Finland-Czechoslovakia: 2-7.
2
The American goalie Marc Behrend.
4
Canada-Soviet Union: 0-4.
5
Soviet Union-Czechoslovakia: 2-0.
7
Swedish players.
8
The Czechoslovak team.
10
Soviet Union-Sweden: 10-1.

161

Sarajevo ´84

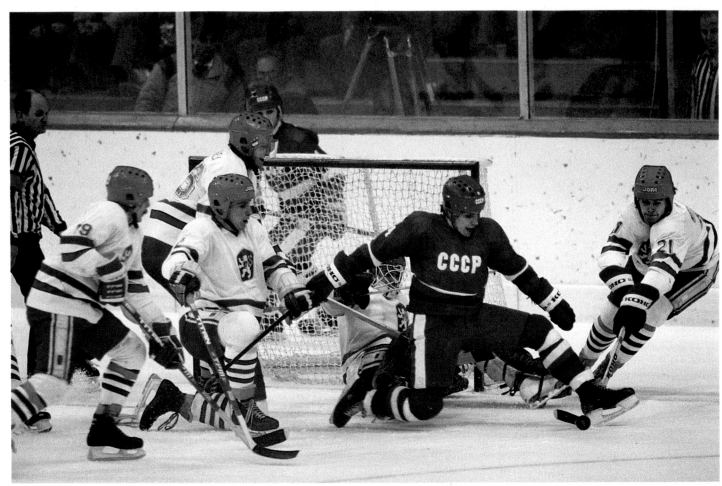

1
Soviet Union-Czechoslovakia, final: 2-0.
2
The goalie Tretyak.

Sarajevo ´84

1
Soviet Union-Sweden: 10-1.
4
Canada-Soviet Union: 0-4.

Sarajevo ´84

1
Finland-Czechoslovakia: 2-7.
3
Czechoslovakia-Canada: 4-0.
4
Canada-USSR: 0-4.
5
Czechoslovakia-Sweden: 2-0.

Sarajevo ´84

1

2

3

2
Czechoslovakia-Sweden: 2-0.
3
Finland-Czechoslovakia: 2-7.

1
Canada-Soviet Union: 0-4.
3
Finland-Czechoslovakia: 2-7.

1
The Swede Ola Rylander. Rylander holds the world
speed record for a handicapped skier at more than
193 km an hour.
2
The 12 medals awarded at Sarajevo.
3
Felix Abele, (FRG).
4
During the opening ceremony.

It's known how energetically the president of the IOC, S.E.M. Juan Antonio Samaranch, has worked to make sport as accessible as possible to the greatest number of people, without forgetting minority groups. It's in this spirit that he founded the Spanish Federation of Sport for the Handicapped.

At Sarajevo, he wanted the participation of the handicapped.

So at the Château de Vidy on February 15, 1983, he met with the people in charge of the Handicapped Sports Federation.

It was a meeting that had been scheduled for Seoul and Calgary. But with the energy and willpower that is so much a part of his character, he brought forward matters more quickly than foreseen: competitions were planned for the handicapped already at Sarajevo.

Thirty-five competitors who were selected at Innsbruck in January, 1984 and who were all top sportsmen were to make the trip to Sarajevo. And on the slopes of Jahorina, forgetful of their handicaps, or rather, making us forget them, they embarked on a giant slalom race just like the others.

Twelve medals were awarded in four categories to those competitors from ten countries whose courage, enthusiasm and joy for life could leave none of us untouched.

Sarajevo ´84

Sarajevo ´84

Oh, those Americans! The Olympic Games at Sarajevo consisted largely of a challenge to the favourites, at least in the realm of alpine skiing. There, the successive postponements of the events wore on the nerves, but the Mahre brothers showed brilliantly how detached they were from these particular events which marked the Games.

On a treacherous course, with an impressive assurance, they added their names to those of Debbie Armstrong and Bill Johnson, two victors who deserve every bit of credit. In Yugoslavia, the Americans excelled not only on snow, but also on ice, notably the phenomenal Scott Hamilton.

Even if the Olympic title holders in ice hockey, the United States, lost, the eight medals won justified a certain satisfaction. Satisfaction can be drawn when looking at the overall results of the Games at Sarajevo. In spite of the worries because of the weather (the nationalist feelings which are inevitable in this kind of circumstances) and the tension caused by the security measures which have become indispensable since Munich, the programme was respected. And for the heroes of this meeting it was a time of the greatest happiness. Marja-Liisa Hämäläinen, the girl from Finland, won three gold medals and one bronze in cross-country skiing. Karin Enke of German Democratic Republic dominated the skating events with two golds and one silver, and Gunde Anders Swan of Sweden won two golds, a silver and a bronze because of his skill at finding the ideal path in cross-country. But do these Games mean something only in terms of metal? At Sarajevo, the joy of the participants, the pride of being together for the most brilliant epic of modern time was enough to banish all doubts. Even if certain skeptics snort at the concept of Olympic spirit by deriding the notion of amateurism, they can't remain insensitive to this display of public enthusiasm. The Yugoslavs through the thoroughness of their organization and the warmth of their welcome won their bet. For the first time, an Eastern country held the winter Olympics. The second, place finish of Jure Franko in the giant slalom, behind Max Julen, that Swiss who showed that Zermatt is not only the Matterhorn but also a region of top skiers, was a suitable repayment. It was the little sentimental touch for those who worked day and night to make sure that the ski slopes were ready in spite of the weather, which, even with all its turbulence, could not disrupt this momentus occasion in Olympism.

Sarajevo ´84

2
Plenty of snow fell on Sarajevo.
3
Sweden's king was an attentive spectator.
4
Sven Tomas Gustafson, silver medal over 10 km and winner of the gold medal over 5 km.
5
Large crowds gathered to watch the jumping events.
6
Vutchko, the Sarajevo Olympics' mascot.

8
Fans from Finland.
9
The American bobsleigh U.S.A. I finished fifth—it had been purchased from Switzerland three days before the race.

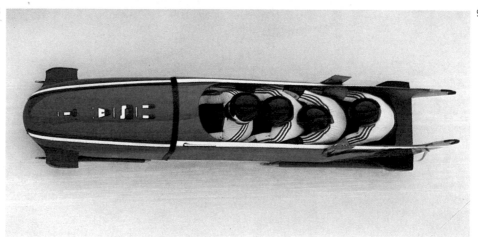

Sarajevo ´84

3
Saunders Alan Sanchez, of Bolivia, eliminated in the
slalom after the second heat.
4
Henrik Bengt Fjaellberg, of Sweden,
disqualified after the second heat.
5
Relaxing at the Olympic Village.

3

4

5

Sarajevo ´84

1
Along with sports, Sarajevo provided a wealth of
cultural and artistic activities.
2
Gunde Anders Swan, four-time medal winner
at Sarajevo.
4
For some people, life continued uneventfully during
the Games.

187

Sarajevo ´84

1
Badges and insignia: trading flourished during the Games.
3
Artists from every part of the country selling their production in the Old Town.

2

3

Sarajevo ´84

1
Shinya Chiba, of Japan, thirtieth in the giant slalom.
2
After dark in Sarajevo.
4
Sarajevo's Olympic Museum.

4

"Hvala Sarajevu... Hvala Jugoslaviji»"

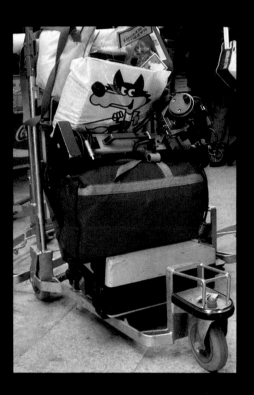

19·2·84

T he Games began with an expression of thanks and they ended with an expression of thanks – a well-deserved one at that.

There's always an element of nostalgia at a closing ceremony, but the production and the enthusiasm of the participants at Sarajovo helped us get over the moment of separation.

On the ice at Zetra, the gathering of Yugoslav youth, the life in this dance of friendship, the two white bears, the mascots for the 1988 Games in Calgary, who joined hands with the little Vuckos, made us forget that the flag with its emblem of five rings had been lowered and the eternal Olympic flame had been extinguished.

The joy of the celebration convinced us that this was only temporary.

Sarajevo ´84

2
The Calgary mascot with young skaters
from Sarajevo.
3
The sadness of the closing doesn't dampen the
enthusiasm of the public.
4
The president of the International Olympic Committee, Juan Antonio Samaranch, thanks Sarajevo and
Yugoslavia for its welcome.
5
Yugoslav youth greet the youth of the whole world.

Sarajevo ´84

2
Juan Antonio Samaranch presents the Olympic
Gold Order to Branko Mikulić, the president of the
organizing committee.
3
Fireworks replace the Eternal Flame.

Sarajevo '84

SPEED SKATING, 10 000 M MEN

1	Malkov, Igor	URS	14:39,90
2	Gustafson, Sven Tomas	SWE	14:39,95
3	Schöfisch, René	GDR	14:46,91
4	Karlstad, Geir	NOR	14:52,40
5	Hadschieff, Michael	AUT	14:53,78
6	Botchkarev, Dimitry	URS	14:55,65
7	Woods, Michael	USA	14:57,30
8	Nilsen, Henry	NOR	14:57,81
9	Kramer, Yep	HOL	14:59,89
10	Van der Duim, Hilbert	HOL	15:01,24

SPEED SKATING, 5000 M MEN

1	Gustafson, Sven Tomas	SWE	7:12,28
2	Malkov, Igor	URS	7:12,30
3	Schöfisch, René	GDR	7:17,49
4	Ehrig, Andreas	GDR	7:17,63
5	Bogiev, Oleg	URS	7:17,96
6	Niittyla, Pertti	FIN	7:17,97
7	Nyland, Björn	NOR	7:18,27
8	Jäger, Werner	AUT	7:18,61
9	Van der Duim, Hilbert	HOL	7:19,39
10	Karlstad, Geir	NOR	7:20,24

SPEED SKATING, 1500 M MEN

1	Boucher, Gaëtan	CAN	1:58,36
2	Khlebnikov, Serguey	URS	1:58,83
3	Bogiev, Oleg	URS	1:58,89
4	Van Helden, Hans	FRA	1:59,39
5	Ehrig, Andreas	GDR	1:59,41
6	Dietel, Andreas	GDR	1:59,73
7	Van der Duim, Hilbert	HOL	1:59,77
8	Chacherin, Victor	URS	1:59,81
9	Niittyla, Pertti	FIN	2:00,01
10	Schalij, Frits	HOL	2:00,14

SPEED SKATING, 1000 M MEN

1	Boucher, Gaëtan	CAN	1:15,80
2	Khlebnikov, Serguey	URS	1:16,63
3	Engelstad, Kai Arne	NOR	1:16,75
4	Thometz, Nick	USA	1:16,85
5	Hoffmann, André	GDR	1:17,33
6	Chacherin, Victor	URS	1:17,42
7	Van der Duim, Hilbert	HOL	1:17,46
8	Dietel, Andreas	GDR	1:17,46
9	Kuroiwa, Akira	JPN	1:17,49
10	Verger, Hein	HOL	1:17,57

SPEED SKATING, 500 M MEN

1	Fokitchev, Serguey	URS	38,19
2	Kitazawa, Yoshihiro	JPN	38,30
3	Boucher, Gaëtan	CAN	38,39
4	Jansen, Dan	USA	38,55
5	Thometz, Nick	USA	38,56
6	Kozlov, Vladimir	URS	38,57
7	Rönning, Frode	NOR	38,58
8	Mey, Jens-Uwe	GDR	38,65
9	Danilin, Alexandre	URS	38,66
10	Kuroiwa, Akira	JPN	38,70

SPEED SKATING, 3000 M WOMEN

1	Schöne, Andrea	GDR	4:24,79
2	Enke, Karin	GDR	4:26,33
3	Schönbrunn, Gabie	GDR	4:33,13
4	Plechkova, Olga	URS	4:34,42
5	Gennip van, Yvonne	HOL	4:34,80
6	Docter, Mary A.	USA	4:36,25
7	Jensen, Björg Eva	NOR	4:36,28
8	Lalenkova, Valentina	URS	4:37,36
9	Petrousseva, Natalya	URS	4:39,36
10	Swider, Nancy	USA	4:40,10

SPEED SKATING, 1500 M WOMEN

1	Enke, Karin	GDR	2:03,42
2	Schöne, Andrea	GDR	2:05,29
3	Petrousseva, Natalya	URS	2:05,78
4	Schönbrunn, Gabie	GDR	2:07,69
5	Rys-Ferens, Erwina	POL	2:08,08
6	Lalenkova, Valentina	URS	2:08,17
7	Kourova, Natalya	URS	2:08,41
8	Jensen, Björg Eva	NOR	2:09,53
9	Limbach, Thea	HOL	2:10,35
10	Smuda, Sigrid	FRG	2:10,55

SPEED SKATING, 1000 M WOMEN

1	Enke, Karin	GDR	1:21,61
2	Schöne, Andrea	GDR	1:22,83
3	Petrousseva, Natalya	URS	1:23,21
4	Lalenkova, Valentina	URS	1:23,68
5	Rothenburger, Christa	GDR	1:23,98
6	Gennip van, Yvonne	HOL	1:25,36
7	Rys-Ferens, Erwina	POL	1:25,81
8	Holzner, Monika	FRG	1:25,87
9	Carlen, Elisabeth	SWE	1:26,15
10	Morawiec, Lilianna	POL	1:26,53

SPEED SKATING, 500 M WOMEN

1	Rothenburger, Christa	GDR	41,02
2	Enke, Karin	GDR	41,28
3	Chive, Natalya	URS	41,50
4	Koulechova, Irina	URS	41,70
5	Walter, Skadi	GDR	42,16
6	Petrousseva, Natalya	URS	42,19
7	Holzner, Monika	FRG	42,40
8	Blair, Bonnie K.	USA	42,53
9	Rys-Ferens, Erwina	POL	42,71
10	Class, Kathryn	USA	42,97

THE FIRST TEN
COMPETITORS IN EACH EVENT

BIATHLON RELAY 4 × 7.5 KM

1	Vassiliev, Dmitry	URS	1.38:51,70
	Kachkarov, Youry		
	Shalna, Alguimantas		
	Bouliguin, Serguey		
2	Lirhus, Odd	NOR	1.39:03,90
	Kvalfoss, Erik		
	Storsveen, Rolf		
	Söbak, Kjell		
3	Reiter, Ernst	FRG	1.39:05,10
	Pichler, Walter		
	Angerer, Peter		
	Fischer, Fritz		
4	Wick, Holger	GDR	1.40:04,70
	Rötsch, Frank-Peter		
	Jacob, Matthias		
	Ullrich, Frank		
5	Darioli, Adriano	ITA	1.42:32,80
	Taschler, Gottlieb		
	Passler, Johann		
	Zingerle, Andreas		
6	Schimunek, Jaromir	TCH	1.42:40,50
	Hak, Zdenek		
	Zelinka, Peter		
	Matousch, Jan		
7	Tiitola, Keijo	FIN	1.43:16,00
	Makikyrö, Toivo		
	Jaaskelainen, Arto		
	Piipponen, Tapio		
8	Horn, Rudolf	AUT	1.43:28,10
	Hörl, Walter		
	Schuler, Franz		
	Eder, Alfred		
9	Mougel, Francis	FRA	1.43:57,60
	Claudon, Eric		
	Mougel, Yvon		
	Poirot, Christian		
10	Fahlen, Sven	SWE	1.44:28,20
	Höglund, Tommy Michael		
	Westling, Roger		
	Adolfsson, Ronnie		

BIATHLON 10 KM

1	Kvalfoss, Erik	NOR	30:53,8
2	Angerer, Peter	FRG	31:02,4
3	Jacob, Matthias	GDR	31:10,5
4	Söbak, Kjell	NOR	31:19,7
5	Shalna, Alguimantas	URS	31:20,8
6	Mougel, Yvon	FRA	31:32,9
7	Rötsch, Frank-Peter	GDR	31:49,8
8	Fischer, Fritz	FRG	32:04,7
9	Matousch, Jan	TCH	32:10,5
10	Kachkarov, Youry	URS	32:15,2

BIATHLON 20 KM

1	Angerer, Peter	FRG	1.11:52,7
2	Rötsch, Frank-Peter	GDR	1.13:21,4
3	Kvalfoss, Erik	NOR	1.14:02,4
4	Mougel, Yvon	FRA	1.14:53,1
5	Ullrich, Frank	GDR	1.14:53,7
6	Storsveen, Rolf	NOR	1.15:23,9
7	Fischer, Fritz	FRG	1.15:49,7
8	Andersson, Leif	SWE	1.16:19,3
9	Zingerle, Andreas	ITA	1.16:21,7
10	Matousch, Jan	TCH	1.16:39,0

COMBINED NORDIC

1	Sandberg, Tom	NOR	422,595
2	Karjalainen, Jouko	FIN	416,900
3	Ylipulli, Jukka	FIN	410,825
4	Miettinen, Rauno	FIN	402,970
5	Müller, Thomas	FRG	401,995
6	Prosvirnin, Alexandre	URS	400,185
7	Dotzauer, Uwe	GDR	397,780
8	Weinbuch, Hermann	FRG	397,390
9	Sulzenbacher, Klaus	AUT	394,570
10	Andersen, Geir	NOR	393,155

70-METRE SKI JUMP

1	Weissflog, Jens	GDR	215,2
2	Nykänen, Matti	FIN	214,0
3	Puikkonen, Jari	FIN	212,8
4	Stannarius, Stefan	GDR	211,1
5	Berg, Rolf Aage	NOR	208,5
6	Felder, Andreas	AUT	205,6
7	Fijas, Piotr	POL	204,5
8	Opaas, Vegard	NOR	203,8
9	Hastings, Jeffrey	USA	203,5
10	Parma, Jiri	TCH	202,7

90-METRE SKI JUMP

1	Nykänen, Matti	FIN	231,2
2	Weissflog, Jens	GDR	213,7
3	Ploc, Pavel	TCH	202,9
4	Hastings, Jeffrey	USA	201,2
5	Puikkonen, Jari	FIN	196,6
6	Kogler, Armin	AUT	195,6
7	Bauer, Andreas	FRG	194,6
8	Podzimek, Vladimir	TCH	194,5
9	Stannarius, Stefan	GDR	188,6
10	Bulau, Horst	CAN	188,3

MEN'S 15 KM CROSS-COUNTRY SKIING

1	Swan, Gunde Anders	SWE	41:25,6
2	Karvonen, Aki	FIN	41:34,9
3	Kirvesniemi, Harri	FIN	41:45,6
4	Mieto, Juha	FIN	42:05,8
5	Nikitin, Vladimir	URS	42:31,6
6	Zimiatov, Nikolay	URS	42:34,5
7	Bellman, Uwe	GDR	42:35,8
8	Holte, Tor Haakon	NOR	42:37,4
9	De Zolt, Maurilio	ITA	42:40,0
10	Batuk, Alexandre	URS	42:42,2

MEN'S 30 KM CROSS-COUNTRY SKIING

1	Zimiatov, Nikolay	URS	1.28:56,3
2	Zavialov, Alexandre	URS	1.29:23,3
3	Swan, Gunde Anders	SWE	1.29:35,7
4	Sakhnov, Vladimir	URS	1.30:30,4
5	Karvonen, Aki	FIN	1.30:59,7
6	Eriksen, Lars Erik	NOR	1.31:24,8
7	Kirvesniemi, Harri	FIN	1.31:37,4
8	Mieto, Juha	FIN	1.31:48,3
9	De Zolt, Maurilio	ITA	1.31:58,7
10	Bellman, Uwe	GDR	1.31:59,3

MEN'S 50 KM CROSS-COUNTRY SKIING

1	Wassberg, Thomas Lars	SWE	2.15:55,8
2	Swan, Gunde Anders	SWE	2.16:00,7
3	Karvonen, Aki	FIN	2.17:04,7
4	Kirvesniemi, Harri	FIN	2.18:34,1
5	Lindvall, Jan Petter	NOR	2.19:27,1
6	Grünenfelder, Andreas	SUI	2.19:46,2
7	Zavialov, Alexandre	URS	2.20:27,6
8	Sakhnov, Vladimir	URS	2.20:53,7
9	Hallenbarter, Konrad	SUI	2.21:11,6
10	Mieto, Juha	FIN	2.21:53,1

WOMEN'S 5 KM CROSS-COUNTRY SKIING

1	Hämäläinen, Marja-Liisa	FIN	17:04,0
2	Aunli, Berit	NOR	17:14,1
3	Jeriova, Kvetoslava	TCH	17:18,3
4	Risby, Lillemor Marie	SWE	17:26,3
5	Nybraaten, Inger Helene	NOR	17:28,2
6	Pettersen, Brit	NOR	17:33,6
7	Jahren, Anne	NOR	17:38,3
8	Noack, Ute	GDR	17:46,0
9	Kratzer, Evi	SUI	17:47,5
10	Maatta, Pirkko	FIN	17:48,0

WOMEN'S 10 KM CROSS-COUNTRY SKIING

1	Hämäläinen, Marja-Liisa	FIN	31:44,2
2	Smetanina, Raissa	URS	32:02,9
3	Pettersen, Brit	NOR	32:12,7
4	Aunli, Berit	NOR	32:17,7
5	Jahren, Anne	NOR	32:26,2
6	Risby, Lillemor Marie	SWE	32:34,6
7	Myrmäl, Marit	NOR	32:35,3
8	Stepanova, Youlia	URS	32:45,7
9	Bourlakova, Nadejda	URS	32:55,8
10	Jeriova, Kvetoslava	TCH	32:58,7

WOMEN'S 20 KM CROSS-COUNTRY SKIING

1	Hämäläinen, Marja-Liisa	FIN	1.01:45,0
2	Smetanina, Raissa	URS	1.02:26,7
3	Jahren, Anne	NOR	1.03:13,6
4	Paulu, Blanka	TCH	1.03:16,9
5	Risby, Lillemor Marie	SWE	1.03:31,8
6	Pettersen, Brit	NOR	1.03:49,0
7	Liadova, Lubov	URS	1.03:53,3
8	Kratzer, Evi	SUI	1.03:56,4
9	Maatta, Pirkko	FIN	1.04:37,6
10	Dal Sasso, Guidina	ITA	1.04:44,1

MEN'S 4 × 10 KM CROSS-COUNTRY RELAY

1	Wassberg, Thomas Lars Kohlberg, Benny Tord Ottosson, Jan Bo Otto Swan, Gunde Anders	SWE	1.55:06,30
2	Batuk, Alexandre Zavialov, Alexandre Nikitin, Vladimir Zimiatov, Nikolay	URS	1.55:16,50
3	Ristanen, Kari Mieto, Juha Kirvesniemi, Harri Karvonen, Aki	FIN	1.56:31,40
4	Eriksen, Lars Erik Lindvall, Jan Petter Aunli, Ove Robert Holte, Tor Haakon	NOR	1.57:27,60
5	Guidon, Giachem Hallenbarter, Konrad Ambühl, Joos Grünenfelder, Andreas	SUI	1.58:06,00
6	Behle, Jochen Dotzler, Stefan Schöbel, Franz Zipfel, Peter	FRG	1.59:30,20
7	De Zolt, Maurilio Runggaldier, Alfred Capitanio, Giulio Vanzetta, Giorgio	ITA	1.59:30,30
8	Simoneau, Dan Caldwell, Timothy J. Galanes, James Koch, Bill	USA	1.59:52,30
9	Brandt, Karsten Wünsch, Uwe Schröder, Frank Bellman, Uwe	GDR	2.02:13,90
10	Atanassov, Svetoslav Simitchiev, Atanas Ivantchev, Milouch Barzanov, Kristo	BUL	2.03:17,60

WOMEN'S 4 × 5 KM CROSS-COUNTRY RELAY

1	Nybraaten, Inger Helene Jahren, Anne Pettersen, Brit Aunli, Berit	NOR	1.06:49,70
2	Schvubova, Dagmar Paulu, Blanka Svobodova, Gabriela Jeriova, Kvetoslava	TCH	1.07:34,70
3	Maatta, Pirkko Hyytiainen, Eija Matikainen, Marjo Hämäläinen, Marja-Liisa	FIN	1.07:36,70
4	Stepanova, Youlia Liadova, Lubov Bourlakova, Nadejda Smetanina, Raissa	URS	1.07:55,00
5	Lamberg, Karin Ingrid Hugosson, Doris Kristina Risby, Lillemor Marie Rosendahl, Ann Janeth	SWE	1.09:30,00
6	Thomas, Karin Germann, Monika Brügger, Christine Kratzer, Evi	SUI	1.09:40,30
7	Long, Susan Rabinowitz, Judy Spencer-Galanes, Lynn Ross, Patricia	USA	1.10:48,40
8	Voge, Petra Rohrmann, Petra Anding, Carola Noack, Ute	GDR	1.11:10,70
9	Angerer, Clara Pozzoni, Paola Di Centa, Manuela Dal Sasso, Guidina	ITA	1.11:12,30
10	Mlakar, Jana Smrekar, Andreja Smolnikar, Tatjana Munih, Metka	YUG	1.13:45,10

It's in every game you play.

MEN'S FIGURE SKATING

1	Hamilton, Scott	USA	3.4
2	Orser, Brian	CAN	5.6
3	Sabovtchik, Jozef	TCH	7.4
4	Cerne, Rudi	FRG	8.2
5	Boitano, Brian	USA	11.0
6	Simond, Christophe J.	FRA	11.8
7	Fadeev, Alexandre	URS	13.2
8	Kotin, Vladimir	URS	16.2
9	Schramm, Norbert	FRG	16.2
10	Fischer, Heiko	FRG	19.6

WOMEN'S FIGURE SKATING

1	Witt, Katarina	GDR	3.2
2	Sumners, Rosalyn	USA	4.6
3	Ivanova, Kira	URS	9.2
4	Chin, Tiffany	USA	11.0
5	Kondracheva, Anna	URS	11.8
6	Zayak, Elaine K.	USA	14.2
7	Ruben, Manuela	FRG	15.0
8	Vodorezova, Elena	URS	15.4
9	Leistner, Claudia	FRG	17.4
10	Dubravcic, Sandra	YUG	17.4

ICE DANCING

1	Torvill, Jayne Dean, Christopher	GBR	2.0
2	Bestemyanova, Natalya Boukin, Andrey	URS	4.0
3	Klimova, Marina Ponomarenko, Serguey	URS	7.0
4	Blumberg, Judy Seibert, Michael	USA	7.0
5	Fox, Carol Dalley, Richard	USA	10.6
6	Barber, Karen Slater, Nicky	GBR	11.4
7	Volojinskaya, Olga Svinin, Alexandre	URS	14.6
8	Wilson, Tracy McCall, Robert	CAN	15.4
9	Born, Petra Schönborn, Rainer	FRG	18.0
10	Spitz, Elisa Gregory, Scott	USA	20.0

PAIRS FIGURE SKATING

1	Valova, Elena Vassiliev, Oleg	URS	1.4
2	Carruthers, Kitty Carruthers, Peter	USA	2.8
3	Selezneva, Larissa Makarov, Oleg	URS	3.8
4	Bäss, Sabine Thierbach, Tassilo	GDR	5.6
5	Lorenz, Birgit Schubert, Knut	GDR	7.0
6	Watson, Jill Lancon, Burt	USA	9.2
7	Underhill, Barbara Martini, Paul	CAN	9.4
8	Matousek, Katerina Eisler, Lloyd	CAN	11.6
9	Avstriyskaya, Marina Kvachnin, Youry	URS	11.8
10	Miller, Lee Ann Fauver, William	USA	14.0

ICE HOCKEY

		Matches	Won	Lost	Goals	Points
1	URS	3	3	0	16: 1	6
2	TCH	3	2	1	6: 2	4
3	SWE	3	1	2	3:12	2
4	CAN	3	0	3	0:10	0
5	FRG	1	1	0	7: 4	2
6	FIN	1	0	1	4: 7	0
7	USA	1	1	0	7: 4	2
8	POL	1	0	1	4: 7	0

WINNERS IN ALL
SPORTS LIGHTING

PHILIPS | 70 m Ski-Jump on Mount Igman at Malo Polje — XIV Olympic Winter Games

Sarajevo '84

MEN'S DOWNHILL

1	Johnson, William D.	USA	1:45,59
2	Müller, Peter	SUI	1:45,86
3	Steiner, Anton	AUT	1:45,95
4	Zurbriggen, Pirmin	SUI	1:46,05
5	Räber, Urs	SUI	1:46,32
6	Höflehner, Helmut	AUT	1:46,32
7	Wildgruber, Sepp	FRG	1:46,53
8	Podborski, Steve	CAN	1:46,59
9	Brooker, Todd	CAN	1:46,64
10	Klammer, Franz	AUT	1:47,04

MEN'S GIANT SLALOM

1	Julen, Max	SUI	2:41,18
2	Franko, Jure	YUG	2:41,41
3	Wenzel, Andreas	LIE	2:41,75
4	Gruber, Franz	AUT	2:42,08
5	Strel, Boris	YUG	2:42,36
6	Strolz, Hubert	AUT	2:42,71
7	Giorgi, Alex	ITA	2:43,00
8	Mahre, Phillip	USA	2:43,25
9	Krizaj, Bojan	YUG	2:43,48
10	Gaspoz, Joël	SUI	2:43,60

MEN'S SLALOM

1	Mahre, Phillip	USA	1:39,41
2	Mahre, Steven	USA	1:39,62
3	Bouvet, Didier	FRA	1:40,20
4	Nilsson, Jonas Lars	SWE	1:40,25
5	Tötsch, Oswald	ITA	1:40,48
6	Popangelov, Petar	BUL	1:40,68
7	Krizaj, Bojan	YUG	1:41,51
8	Halvarsson, Lars-Göran	SWE	1:41,70
9	Strand, Stig	SWE	1:41,95
10	Bürgler, Thomas	SUI	1:42,03

WOMEN'S DOWNHILL

1	Figini, Michela	SUI	1:13,36
2	Walliser, Maria	SUI	1:13,41
3	Charvatova, Olga	TCH	1:13,53
4	Ehrat, Ariane	SUI	1:13,95
5	Gantnerova, Jana	TCH	1:14,14
6	Kiehl, Marina	FRG	1:14,30
7	Sorensen, Gerry	CAN	1:14,30
8	Sölkner, Lea	AUT	1:14,39
9	Kirchler, Elisabeth	AUT	1:14,55
10	Wallinger, Veronika	AUT	1:14,76

WOMEN'S GIANT SLALOM

1	Armstrong, Debbie	USA	2:20,98
2	Cooper, Christin	USA	2:21,38
3	Pelen, Perrine	FRA	2:21,40
4	McKinney, Tamara P.	USA	2:21,83
5	Kiehl, Marina	FRG	2:22,03
6	Fernandez-Ochoa, Blanca	ESP	2:22,14
7	Hess, Erika	SUI	2:22,51
8	Charvatova, Olga	TCH	2:22,57
9	Savijarvi, Liisa	CAN	2:22,73
10	Rey, Anne-Flore	FRA	2:22,95

WOMEN'S SLALOM

1	Magoni, Paoletta	ITA	1:36,47
2	Pelen, Perrine	FRA	1:37,38
3	Konzett, Ursula	LIE	1:37,50
4	Steiner, Roswitha	AUT	1:37,84
5	Hess, Erika	SUI	1:37,91
6	Tlalka, Malgorzata	POL	1:37,97
7	Quario, Maria Rosa	ITA	1:37,99
8	Kronbichler, Anni	AUT	1:38,05
9	Zini, Daniela	ITA	1:38,15
10	Charvatova, Olga	TCH	1:38,66

Measuring the Olympians

Only one country
was asked to send <u>two</u> teams to Sarajevo:
Switzerland.

The second Swiss team were the 70 timekeepers of the Swiss Timing organisation who travelled to the Winter Olympics with several million dollars worth of hyper-sophisticated electronic gear.

Their job: to measure Olympic performances to 1/1000th second.
You might say that every score at Sarajevo came with the "Made in Switzerland" guarantee.

Olympic athletes like that guarantee; so much that Swiss Timing and its partners – Longines and Omega – will be reporting for work also at Los Angeles.

 LONGINES   *SWISS TIMING*   Ω OMEGA

Official Timekeeper of the Olympic Games

Sarajevo '84

FOUR-MAN BOB

1	Hoppe, Wolfgang Wetzig, Roland Schauerhammer, Dietmar Kirchner, Andreas	GDR I	3:20,22
2	Lehmann, Bernhard Musiol, Bogdan Voge, Ingo Weise, Eberhard	GDR II	3:20,78
3	Giobellina, Silvio Stettler, Heinz Salzmann, Urs Freiermuth, Rico	SUI I	3:21,39
4	Fasser, Ekkehard Märchy, Hans Poletti, Kurt Strittmatter, Rolf	SUI II	3:22,90
5	Jost, Jeffrey Briski, Joseph Barnes, Thomas Hoye, Hal Andrew	USA I	3:23,33
6	Kipurs, Janis Poikans, Matis Berzups, Incars Chnepsts, Aivar	URS I	3:23,51
7	Degan, Dotin Popescu, Cornel Lixandru, Georghe Petrariu, Costel	ROM I	3:23,76
8	Ghedina, Guerrino Ticci, Stefano Scaramuzza, Paolo Meneghin, Andrea	ITA II	3:23,77
9	Kopp, Klaus Öchsle, Gerhard Neuburger, Gunther Schummacher, Hans-Joachim	FRG I	3:24,15
10	Delle-Karth, Walter Krispel, Gunter Grössing, Ferdinand Lindner, Hans	AUT I	3:24,21

TWO-MAN BOB

1	Hoppe, Wolfgang Schauerhammer, Dietmar	GDR II	3:25,56
2	Lehmann, Bernhard Musiol, Bogdan	GDR I	3:26,04
3	Ekmanis, Zintis Aleksandrov, Vladimir	URS II	3:26,16
4	Kipurs, Janis Chnepsts, Aivar	URS I	3:26,42
5	Hiltebrand, Hans Müller, Meinhard	SUI I	3:26,76
6	Pichler, Ralph Freiermuth, Rico	SUI II	3:28,23
7	Ghedina, Guerrino Meneghin, Andrea	ITA I	3:29,09
8	Fischer, Anton Metzler, Hans	FRG I	3:29,18
9	Bellodis, Marco Ticci, Stefano	ITA II	3:30,02
10	Lloyd Malcolm Brugnani, Peter	GBR II	3:30,36

MEN'S DOUBLE LUGE

1	Stangassinger, Hans Wembacher, Franz	FRG	1:23,620
2	Beloussov, Evgueny Belyakov, Alexandar	URS	1:23,660
3	Hoffmann, Joerg Pietzsch, Jochen	GDR	1:23,887
4	Fluckinger, Georg Wilhemer, Franz	AUT	1:23,902
5	Lemmerer, Günther Lechleitner, Franz	AUT	1:24,133
6	Raffl, Hansjorg Huber, Norbert	ITA	1:24,353
7	Eyssak, Yuris Veykcha, Eynar	URS	1:24,366
8	Schwab, Thomas Staudinger, Wolfgang	FRG	1:24,634
9	Rossi, Ronald Bateman, Douglas	USA	1:24,651
10	Brunner, Helmut Brunner, Walter	ITA	1:24,788

MEN'S SINGLE LUGE

1	Hildgartner, Paul	ITA	3:04,258
2	Danilin, Serguev	URS	3:04,962
3	Doudin, Valerij	URS	3:05,012
4	Walter, Michael	GDR	3:05,031
5	Görlitzer, Torsten	GDR	3:05,129
6	Haspinger, Ernst	ITA	3:05,327
7	Khartchenko, Youri	URS	3:05,548
8	Prock, Markus	AUT	3:05,839
9	Huber, Norbert	ITA	3:05,909
10	Sandbichler, Gerhard	AUT	3:06,453

WOMEN'S SINGLE LUGE

1	Martin, Steffi	GDR	2:46,570
2	Schmidt, Bettina	GDR	2:46,873
3	Weiss, Ute	GDR	2:47,248
4	Amantova, Ingrida	URS	2:48,480
5	Zozoulya, Vera	URS	2:48,641
6	Rainer, Maria-Luise	ITA	2:49,138
7	Göllner, Annefried	AUT	2:49,373
8	Hatle, Andrea	FRG	2:49,491
9	Zeitz, Constanze	FRG	2:49,836
10	Licitsa, Natalya	URS	2:50,087

YASSA®

Opening Ceremony: Yassa Styles Everywhere.

Official International Olympic Committee book SARAJEVO '84

Conception and Production
STUDIO 6, Lausanne

Direction
Goran TAKAČ

Administration and Coordination
Jean-Claude WIDMER

Graphics
STUDIO 6, Lausanne
artistic director: Stéphane ORRIÈRE

Exclusive photos
STUDIO 6, Lausanne:
Mihajlo ANTIĆ
David CANNON
Kosta CVETIČANIN
Milan DJURICA
Slobodan DJUROVIĆ
Alain GAVILLET, A.S.L.
Slobodan JEVTOVIĆ
Mete RAZLIKLI, A.S.L.
Goran TAKAČ
Calle TÖRNSTRÖM

Texts
International Olympic Committee:
Frille ERIKSSON
Alexandra STEVENSON
Edward SWIFT
André Mercé VARELA
Jean-Claude WIDMER
Bertrand ZIMMERMANN

Translations
Hans U. AEBERSOLD
Alfie ANDERSON
Pierre MONGEAU
Paul SUFRIN
Charlie WEDIN

Photolitho
NT PRINT

Special thanks to
Juan Antonio SAMARANCH,
president IOC
Branko MIKULIĆ,
president of the Yugoslav
Olympic Organizing Committee
Monique BERLIOUX,
director IOC
Albert G. RIETHAUSEN
Matti SALMENKYLÄ
Bob FERRIER
Ivica MIŠIĆ
Dragan STEFANOVIĆ
Etienne GAULIS
Guy PRINCIVALLE

All photos were made with Kodak-Ektachrome film
and developed at Kodak laboratories at Sarajevo
in three hours.
The cameras and the lenses were made by Nikon,
the official camera of the Olympic Games,
Sarajevo '84.